I KNOW WHO JESUS IS

Written and Illustrated by
Helen Caswell

Lutterworth Press
Cambridge

First published by Lutterworth Press 1989
Copyright © by Abingdon Press
All Rights Reserved
This book is printed on acid-free paper.
British Library Cataloguing in Publication data available
ISBN 0 7188 2795 3

MANUFACTURED IN HONG KONG

To Jessica Caswell

Lots of times
I wonder about Jesus,
and how he lived on earth
a long time ago.
I wish I could have been there.

Jesus came as a little baby
so that he could be born like one
of us and live with us
here for a while.

Jesus grew up
just like other boys.
Only, of course,
he was a lot more special.

Jesus liked sheep,
and he liked the shepherds
who took care of the little lambs.

He liked boats, too, and fishermen.

Sometimes they had barbecues on the beach.

One time Jesus made a storm stop
because the fishermen were afraid.
He told them they must not be afraid,
because he was with them.

Even though Jesus had all the power of God,
he didn't go around moving mountains or anything like that.
He used his power for helping people.
He cured people who were sick
and made blind people see again.
Once a little girl was so sick she died,
but Jesus brought her back to life.

One day a lot of people
came to hear Jesus talk.
It was dinner time but there was
hardly anything to eat.
Jesus took a few loaves of bread
and some little fish that a boy had brought
and turned them into enough food
to feed all those people.

I wish I had been that boy.

Jesus liked little children a lot.

And the children liked him, too.

He would hold them on his lap
and tell them stories.
I wish I could sit on Jesus' lap.

Even though Jesus went to heaven,
he's not very far away.
I can talk to him,
and sometimes I can almost feel
his hand in mine.

I know Jesus loves me.

God Must Like to Laugh teaches children about God and the world God created.

I Know Who Jesus Is tells children about Jesus and his life.

My Big Family at Church helps children understand church and why we go.

THE GROWING IN · FAITH LIBRARY

The Growing in Faith Library presents these beautifully illustrated books by Helen Caswell. They are designed to introduce children to the basic concepts of the Christian faith.

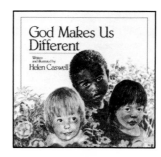

God Makes Us Different shows children that all of us are beautiful and special in God's eyes.

All titles are available from Lutterworth Press.

I Can Talk with God shows children how they can pray and listen to God.

God's Love Is for Sharing explains how we can share God's love with others.

God Is Always with Me helps children understand eternal life.